CHESTNUT THE PUP

WHAT I WOULD SAY IF I COULD TALK

Based on a True Character by Anelda L. Attaway

Story and Pictures by Anelda L. Attaway

Hello, I'm Chestnut! I love my human mommy and daddy and they love me too! I can't speak to them with human words,

Every morning when I wake up I check on mom and dad. I run to their bed side and then I give my tail a wag. When I see that they are OK I'm ready to play! If I could talk I would say,

GOOD MORNING, I'M READY TO START MY DAY.

I know my parents think they always know how I feel. They think I'm unhappy or bored when I lay down or sit still, but If I could talk I would say,

Sometimes I bark to warn mom and dad when someone's at the door, or when I'm feeling hungry, or have to potty and go outdoors. If I could talk instead of bark I would simply say,

I'M TRYING TO LET YOU KNOW MOM AND DAD I NEED TO DO THESE THINGS RIGHT AWAY!

Sometimes I whine and make a squeaky noise to try and get my way. If I could talk I'd say,

During the day mom and dad do something called cleaning. I watch them do this boring thing and wonder, what's the meaning? If I could talk I'd say,

TAKE A BREAK, SO WE CAN PLAY, OR GO FOR A WALK, OR RUN, LET'S DO SOMETHING FUN TODAY!

I'm always happy when I see my parents, so I do flips and jumps, but when I see them reach for my puppy gate I get sad and down in the dumps. If I could talk I would say,

PLEASE DON'T LOCK ME BEHIND THE GATE. I'D RATHER BE FREE TO RUN AND PLAY. I WISH I COULD ESCAPE!

I also am not happy when I have to go in my crate, but if I could talk I'd say,

Sometimes I wait patiently at home, until my parents finish all they have to do. If I could talk I would say,

There are lots of things my parent's do that brings me so much joy. Like asking me to do a trick or calling me Good Boy. One of my favorite parts of the day when they reach for my treats!

Even before the bag is open and I'm jumping on my feet! If I could talk I would yell out,

Sometimes my room gets messy and someone makes it clean. If I could talk I would say,

I LIKED IT BETTER THE MESSY WAY WITH ALL MY SCATTERED THINGS.

Because I'm a puppy I look for things to chew. If I could talk I would say,

I look for shoes every day and drag them in my crate, but mommy always catches me and takes them away. If I could talk I'd tell my mom,

I'M SORRY I WAS BAD, BUT THOSE SHOES I TAKE AND CHEW ARE THE BEST TOYS I EVER HAD.

When she takes the shoes away, she puts them way up high. If I could talk I would say, "I wish that I could fly!"

My parents feed me twice a day and give me plenty of water to drink.

And if I could talk I would say, "More gravy please!"

I like doing things my mommy does, like watching the TV. If I could talk sometimes I'd say,

I love having my mommy close to me. She is warm, tender, and sweet. She holds me, pets me, and cuddles me till I doze off to sleep. If I could talk I'd tell her,

I LOVE BEING IN YOUR ARMS. YOU MAKE ME FEEL SO LOVED AND SAFE FROM ANY HARM.

Daddy does a fantastic job grooming me. He brushes me every day. He also gives me a bath. If I'd could talk I'd say,

THANKS DAD FOR KEEPING ME NICE AND CLEAN! I LOVE THE SHAMPOO MASSAGES, THEY MAKE JUST LIKE A KING!

After I take my bath, dad towels and blow dries me with care. If I could talk I'd say,

I get brushed daily and my daddy does it from his heart. If I could talk I'd say,

I'm so happy my mom and dad brought me home with them to stay. They chose me out of all the other puppies and if I could talk I'd say,

Mommy and daddy in our home is where I want to stay. If I could talk I'd say,

MEET CHESTNUT THE PUP AND HIS FAMILY

Chestnut has a loving family. Anelda is his mommy, Kevin is his daddy, and he has a big sister named Moe. Chestnut's family is passionate about animals and they are advocating against animal cruelty with this book.

They encourage pet rescue and adoption because they believe that every pet deserves a family to love and care for them responsibly.

Chestnut's mommy Anelda wrote this book to share her wonderful pup with the world and to show that animals have their own way to communicate and express themselves. Chestnut and his family would love for you to share this book with a new pet owner or animal lover close to your heart! Most importantly, give it some thought about what your pet would say if they could talk.

This book is dedicated to my father **the late Cleveland Scott Jr.** He loved this book! Daddy, your love, dedication, wise advice, and encouragement will be missed. The smile on your face when you first saw this book will always be remembered.

Also, to my loving husband **Kevin Attaway** and our pup **Chestnut** for their love and support! Chestnut was a gift to Kevin for his 40th birthday!!! Chestnut has changed our lives!

Special thanks to **Moe** for helping with the family picture.

To my loving sister **Larenda Francis** for suggesting we get a puppy from **Patience's Puppies.** They located in Townsend, Delaware. All of their puppies are Veterinarian checked. Their motto is: **Bring Me Home A Happy and Healthy Puppy.**

Chestnut the Pup, What I Would Say If I Could Talk

Published by Jazzy Kitty Publications Formerly Jazzy Kitty Publishing

19 Lukens Drive, New Castle, DE 19720

877.782.5550 - http://www.jazzykittypublications.com

Written by Anelda L. Attaway (Original Poetry) – Paperback version

Book review and Co-editor: Angel Charlemagne

ISBN: 978-1-7324523-1-2

Library of Congress Control Number: 2018906904

Additional Credits: Book Cover created and designed by: Sydney Durrah, Logo Designs by: Andre M. Saunders and Leroy Grayson. Artwork/Illustrations/Front Cover Picture of Chestnut created by Anelda Attaway utilizing Artista, inCollage, and Lunna Design. Webster's Dictionary for the glossary.

Photos: Anelda L. Attaway and Patience's Puppies featuring Chestnut Attaway.

Copyright © 2018 Anelda L. Attaway Jazzy Kitty Publications. All rights explicitly reserved worldwide. This book is protected under the copyright laws of the United States of America. This book may not be copied or reprinted for commercial profit or net income. The purpose of short quotations or occasional page copying for personal or group study is permitted and promoted. Permission to copy will be freely granted upon request. For Worldwide Distribution. Printed and published in the United States of America. Created Jazzy Kitty Greetings Marketing & Publishing, LLC dba Jazzy Kitty Publications Formerly Jazzy Kitty Publishing utilizing Microsoft Publishing Software, Arista, InCollage, and Lunna Design. Paperback version.

Glossary – Words to Know

Abuse–misuse: treat (a person or an animal) with cruelty or violence, especially regularly or repeatedly.

Actions–something done or performed; act; deed.

Among–in, in the midst of, surrounded by.

Assume–to take for granted or without proof.

Attention–notice or awareness.

Barely–almost not.

Bored–to weary by dullness, tiresome.

Glossary – Words to Know

Chew–to crush, damage, injure, grind with the teeth.

Chill–to calm down, take a break.

Communicate–to give or interchange thoughts, feelings by writing and/or speaking.

Contain–to keep under proper control; restrain.

Constant–regularly recurrent; continual; persistent.

Content–happy, satisfied.

Glossary – Words to Know

Cuddling–to hold close in an affectionate manner; hug tenderly.

Dedicated–to offer formally a book or a piece of music to a person, show affection or respect, as on a prefatory page.

Discover–to see, get knowledge of, learn about, or find out.

Drag–pull heavily or slowly along.

Eventually–finally; at some later time.

Flip–to cause to turn over in the air.

Glossary – Words to Know

Groomed–to clean, brush, and otherwise tend to.

Locked up–securing a door, gate, drawer, closed.

Messy–dirty, untidy, or in a disordered condition.

Quickly–with speed; rapidly; very soon.

Relax–to seek rest.

Squeak–a short, sharp, shrill cry; a high-pitched sound.

Whine–to utter a low, usually nasal, complaining cry or sound, as from uneasiness, discontent, or irritability.

www.ingramcontent.com/pod-product-compliance
Lightning Source LLC
Chambersburg PA
CBHW041119070526
44584CB00002B/217